21123311E

TS

This book is to be returned on or before
the date stamped below.

HOCKEY

Gill Lloyd
and
David Jefferis

Wayland

SPORTS SKILLS

Titles in this series:

Cricket	Netball
Gymnastics	Rugby Union
Hockey	Soccer
Judo	Tennis

Photographs by Action Plus, AllSport and P. Luck
Illustrations by James Robins and Drawing Attention
Consultant Mike Hamilton, Director of Coaching, Hockey Association

First published in 1993 by
Wayland (Publishers) Ltd
61 Western Road, Hove
East Sussex BN3 1JD, England

British Library Cataloguing in Publication Data
Lloyd, Gill
  Hockey. - (Sports Skills Series)
  I. Title II. Jefferis, David
  III. Robins, James IV. Series
  796.35

ISBN 0-7502-0980-1

DTP by The Design Shop
Printed and bound in Italy by G. Canale & C.S.p.A., Turin

Contents

Introduction

Hockey is a fast and furious game played by two teams of eleven players. Each side tries to move a hockey ball up the pitch and into the opposing goal, touching the ball only with hockey sticks. The eleven opponents do all they can to stop such attacks and try to take possession of the ball to score goals themselves. The team that scores most goals wins the match.

▽ The high speed at which the ball moves means that the game is played at a very fast pace. The rules of hockey are designed to encourage an athletic, skilful and safe game.

Hockey can be played by men and women, girls and boys. At top levels, the game calls for supreme fitness and high degrees of skill. Traditionally, hockey has been played on grass pitches, but artificial grass is now often used, making the pace of an already fast-moving sport still faster. Despite its popularity, hockey remains an amateur game. The top international teams compete in the Olympics, the World Cup, and regional competitions such as the European Championships.

△ Hockey can be adapted to suit all sorts of levels and age groups. Most hockey is played by single-sex teams, as in the children's game shown here, but some clubs now play mixed hockey, with both boys and girls playing on the same side.

Getting started

Hockey is a popular game in many girls' schools, though it is less common for boys to play at school. Even if you are lucky enough to learn hockey at school, you will probably want to join a club to get regular coaching and good competition. Many clubs run mini-hockey (under-12), colts (under-14) as well as senior and veteran (over-35) hockey.

Clothes worn by most of the players are simple and inexpensive. A shirt, shorts or a skirt and football-style socks are all you need. On grass, the best footwear is a pair of good quality soccer boots. Feet and ankles need firm support because in this game of start, stop, turn and sprint, footwear must fit well.

◁ If you play on a synthetic surface such as Astroturf, training shoes with pimpled soles can be worn. Shinguards, made from lightweight plastic or foam, must be worn underneath socks to protect shins and ankles from knocks. Gum shields should also be worn.

◁ The goalkeeper must wear special protection to guard against the impact of balls fired at the goal. The usual equipment includes a helmet and visor, padded gloves, thigh pads and leg-guards. Kickers are worn over the shoes. They are shaped so they mould to the foot. Other essential items include a chest protector, and a box for men and boys.

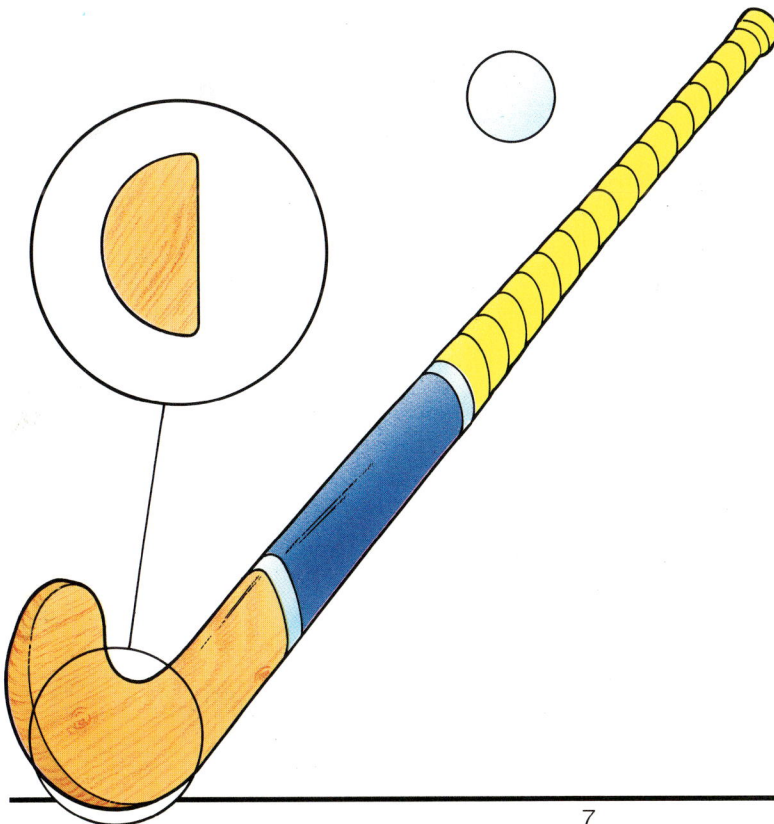

◁ The hockey ball is hard and weighs between 156g and 163g. Young players use a lightweight ball.

◁ The left-hand face of a hockey stick is flat. You strike the ball with the flat, whether you are left or right-handed. The rounded back of the stick cannot be used to play the ball.

It is important to buy a stick of the correct length, so that your swing feels comfortable. As a guide, the tip of the handle should touch your hips when the head of the stick is on the ground.

Rules and umpires

A goal is scored when the ball passes completely over the goal-line, between the posts and under the crossbar, provided it has been hit (or deflected off an attacker's stick) from within the shooting circle (the 'D'). The person who hits the ball can be outside the shooting circle as long as the ball itself is inside.

Two umpires control the game, usually following play from the sides of the pitch. They each cover one half of the pitch and use a whistle to signal fouls, and when the ball has passed out of the field of play. A full game consists of two 35-minute periods, with a five-minute interval, during which teams change ends.

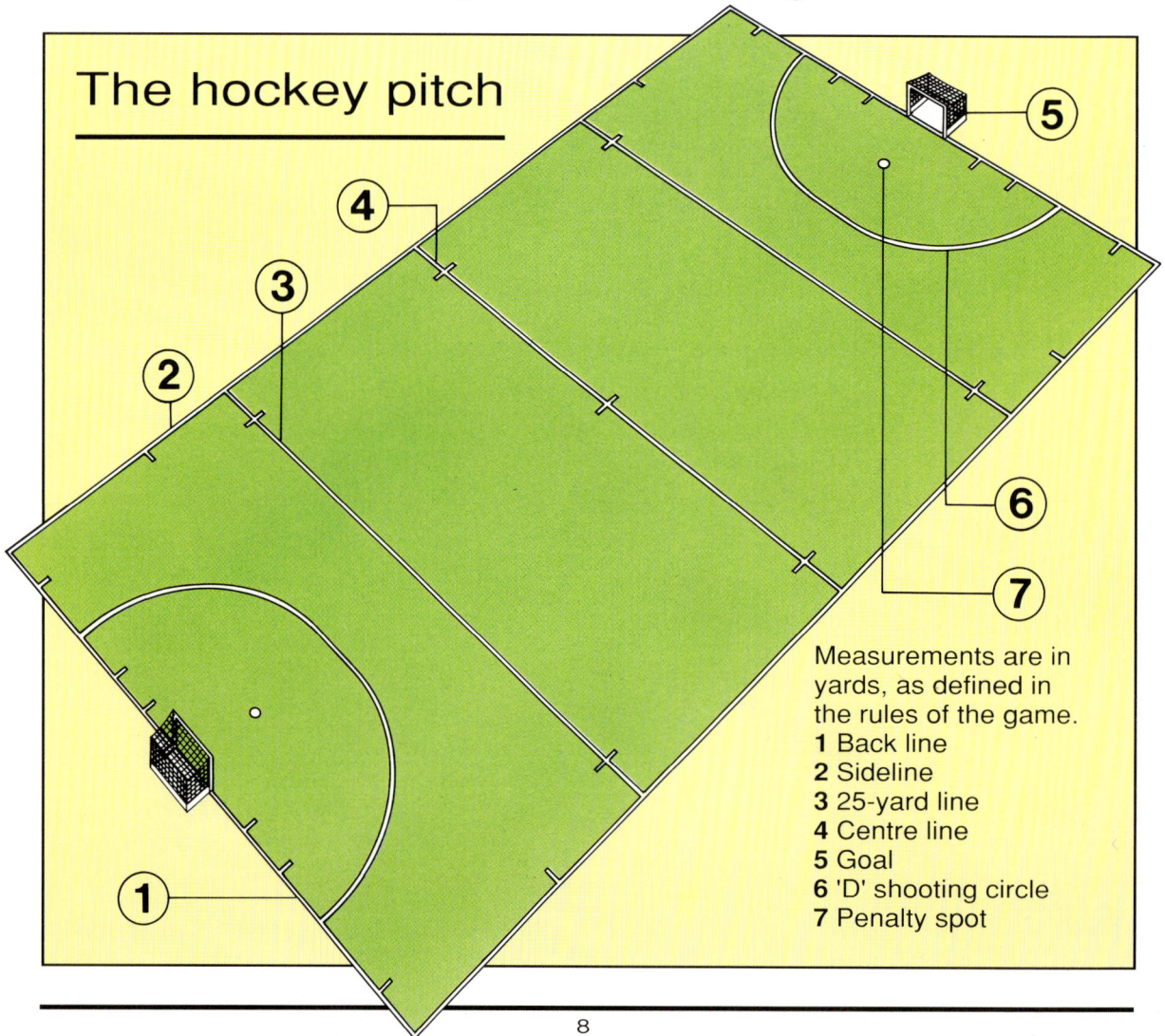

The hockey pitch

Measurements are in yards, as defined in the rules of the game.
1 Back line
2 Sideline
3 25-yard line
4 Centre line
5 Goal
6 'D' shooting circle
7 Penalty spot

There are a number of rules that need to be followed during play. You must use the face of the stick to hit the ball. The ball cannot be stopped by hands, feet, legs or any other part of the body, unless you are the goalkeeper. You must always use a stick and if you drop it or break it you cannot take part in play.

Dangerous play with the stick, such as swinging it wildly in a crowded area, is a serious offence. You also commit a foul if you hit the ball dangerously, for example, through the air, towards a group of players.

△ A foul tackle. Tackling is part of the game, but you are not allowed to hit, hold or interfere with an opponent's stick. Neither can you shove, kick or strike an opponent.

Team play

Teams are made up of eleven players, one of whom is the goalkeeper. There are a mixture of attacking players, midfield players and defenders in a side, but in the best teams, players work together rather than trying to play just as individuals. Learning to position yourself effectively on the field is one of the skills of hockey. Different positions have different roles and these change depending on the tactics of the team.

Formations

Team formations are ways of arranging players as an effective unit. One of the basic formations is '5-3-2-1', meaning that there are five forwards, three midfielders and two defenders in front of the goalkeeper. This formation is shown in the top half of the pitch shown on the right.

1 Goalkeeper
2 Left full back
3 Right full back
4 Right half
5 Centre half
6 Left half
7 Inside right
8 Inside left
9 Right wing
10 Centre forward
11 Left wing.

The triangles that are formed by these positions give good support to the player with the ball and good cover against an attack from the other side.

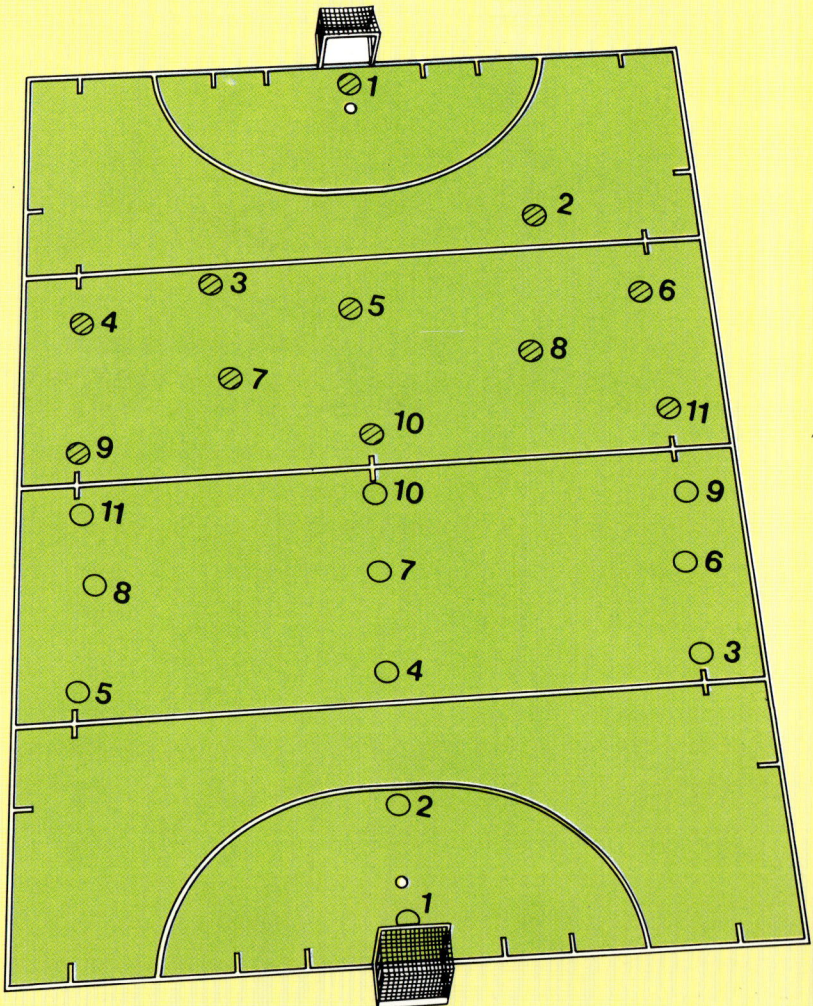

▷ Marking is a vital skill in defence and a part of good team play. Players mark their opposite numbers, try to shadow them and prevent them from receiving or passing the ball.

However, be aware that there is a difference between tight marking and obstruction!

The '3-3-3-1-1' formation is used in more senior hockey. It is a system that is highly effective for marking members of the other side. This formation is shown on the lower half of the pitch shown on the left.

1 Goalkeeper
2 Sweeper
3 Right back
4 Centre back
5 Left back
6 Right midfield
7 Centre midfield
8 Left midfield
9 Right striker
10 Centre striker
11 Left striker

16 players can make up a team, with only 11 allowed on the pitch at any one time. A player who has been substituted may come back on for another player.

Players can go anywhere on the field, but you will be penalized for 'offside' if you are in your opponents' 25-yard area and closer to the goal-line than the ball, unless there are at least two members of the other team nearer to the goal-line than you. One of these may be their goalkeeper. You won't necessarily be penalized for being offside though, unless you try to play the ball or the ball is being passed to you.

Running with the ball

Running down the field with the ball under control is called dribbling. It is a basic skill of hockey that you can practise on your own with a stick and ball. During a game, you will find dribbling a useful way of moving play away from your opponents' defence or getting out of a difficult situation into open space. If you find yourself with plenty of time and space and no opponents nearby, you can run with the ball down the field at high speed.

◁ In the forehand, or open-sided dribble, the ball is kept on the right-hand side of your body, in front of your right shoulder and just outside your right foot. Keep stick and ball ahead of your feet, so you can run easily and see where you are going. Keep your stick in fairly close contact with the ball.

△ Whether you are right-handed or left-handed you use the same grip. The left hand should be at the top of the stick, the right about one-third of the way down the handle. The right hand provides power to strokes, the left twists and turns the stick.

The distance between your hands changes, depending on the type of stroke being used and the distance of the ball from your body. For example, both hands are close together at the top of the stick for a hit.

You can turn the stick in your hands so that the flat side is on the right of the stick. This is known as 'reverse stick' and is used to stop balls coming to you on your left-hand side. Reverse stick can also be used when you are dribbling with the ball, moving it from side to side in front of you while on the move. The technique is known as the 'Indian Dribble'.

△ Sometimes it is useful to move the ball from left to right. To do this you need to turn the stick so that the flat side faces right - this is known as 'reverse stick'.

Passing skills 1

Passes

Three of the most common types of pass are shown in these diagrams.

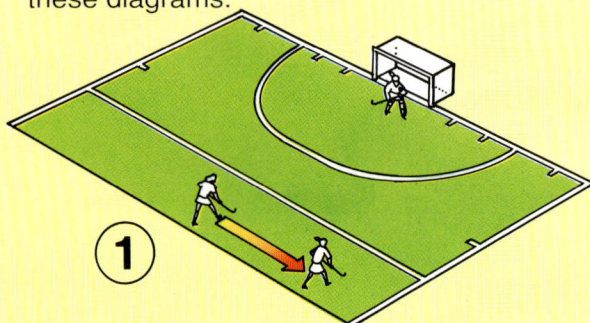

1

A square pass is made at an angle of about 90 degrees to the sidelines.

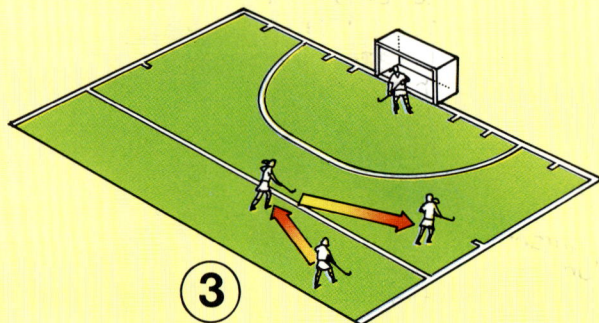

2

Through passes are those made roughly parallel with the sidelines.

3

Angled passes are those made at acute angles across the field.

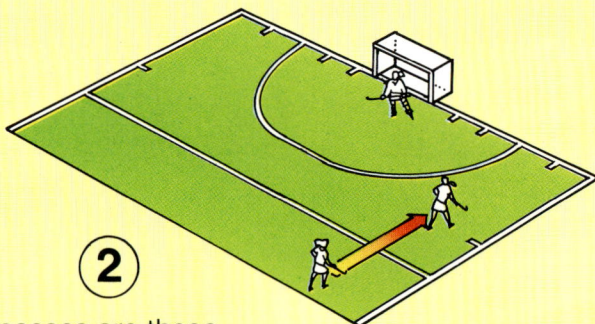

The main way of moving the ball down the hockey field is by passing it. Making successful passes is not easy. You need to be able to hit, push or flick the ball right to the stick of a team-mate. You have to judge both the direction and the speed of a pass.

Basic passing skills are pushing, hitting and flicking (aerial passes). All passes are side-on skills. When you make a pass, turn and point your shoulder towards the direction of the stroke. For forehand or 'open stick' shots it is the left shoulder, for reverse stick shots the right. Deception is also an important part of passing, for if you can disguise your next move, the surprise factor will make it even more effective.

▷ The open stick or forehand push pass is the most accurate way of passing the ball over short distances. Use a grip with hands apart, stand sideways-on to the ball with your left shoulder and left foot pointing towards where you are aiming. Your feet should be a little more than shoulder width apart, knees slightly bent. Move your body weight from right to left foot as you push the ball, keeping the stick in contact with the ball for as long as possible. Then follow through in the direction of the stroke.

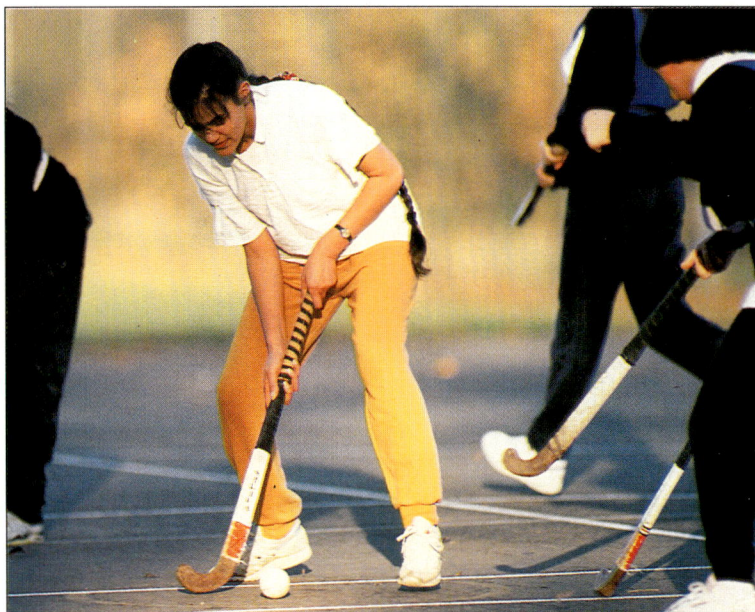

Push pass

A low body position and strong follow-through produce a powerful stroke. To put yet more power into the push, start the shot from further behind the ball. This is known as a 'slap'.

Reverse push

The reverse-stick push is played with the stick in the reverse position, to pass the ball from left to right over short distances. The shot is played the same way as the forehand push, but in reverse. The right shoulder and foot point in the direction of the pass.

Passing skills 2

◁ In the forehand hit, your right hand slides up the stick, close to your left hand. Stand side-on, with your left shoulder pointing in the direction of hit, your feet apart, knees slightly bent. The ball should be near the toes of your left foot.

Keeping your eyes on the ball, take the stick back, then sweep it to the ball with your arms straight. Transfer your weight to your left leg at the moment of impact. Follow through along the line of the ball.

The powerful hit is used to send the ball over longer distances or to shoot at goal. Hitting the ball from left to right is quite difficult, unless you twist your body so that your shoulder points in the direction in which you wish to hit the ball.

Overhead or aerial passes are useful shots for lifting the ball and dropping it behind the opposition defence. Top players are able to lift the ball, to pass it more than 50 metres. However, if you use one of these shots in a manner that will put other players in danger, you will be penalized.

The flick is an important shot in play as well as for penalty strokes (see pages 26/27). The grip and body position are the same as those for the push, but the ball is best positioned a little further ahead, so that you can get the stick under the ball as you flick it. Your body should be a little lower as you do so.

△ For the flick, transfer your weight from right to left foot as you lift the ball up and forward (**1**). Follow-through (**2**) determines the height and path of the ball. The skill of the flick is in keeping the stick in contact with the ball for as long as possible, held as far away from the body as you can.

◁ For scoops you must keep your body very low until the ball has left the stick. The scoop is a shovelling action, your right shoulder brought forward.

Receiving the ball

If passing the ball is an important part of the game, then the skills of receiving and controlling passes quickly are just as vital.

The receiver should try to be in a balanced position when collecting a pass, watching the ball right on to the stick. The right hand should 'give' as the ball makes contact with the stick, to absorb the impact energy. Move into the line of an approaching ball and try to stay on that line as long as possible.

△ Players wait eagerly, ready to receive a free hit. The player in red is hoping to trap the ball with a flat stick, the others have their sticks upright. The ball is received close to the right foot, with the stick face angled towards the ground.

Receiving a straight ball

Keep your body in line with the ball, knees bent, head over it. Grip the stick with your left hand at the top, right hand halfway down the shaft. Hold the stick upright inclined slightly forward. Watch the ball right on to the stick. The right hand should give as the ball contacts the stick.

From the left

Allow the ball to come across in front of your body. Control it in front of your right foot. Get your eyes, stick and body behind the line of the ball.

From the right

Passes from the right can be taken with an open or reversed stick. The choice depends on the next move the receiver is planning. Taking the ball with a reversed stick enables you to move ahead easily once you have the ball. As the ball comes from your right, let it pass across in front of your body. Control it when it is in front of or just outside your left foot. Use your left wrist to turn the stick and line up your head with the ball, keeping your body weight well forward.

Game skills in attack

When you have possession of the ball you have to make a decision about whether you will dribble past an opponent or make a pass. 'Vision' is the name given to the ability to assess what is going on over the rest of the pitch, while judging your distance from an opponent and taking in details such as the position of his or her stick or feet.

Changes of pace, both slowing down and speeding up, can be very effective in beating an opponent. Another tactic to use is deception. If you give the impression you are moving in one direction, then when your opponent is committed, suddenly dodge the other way, you can throw him or her off-balance. When you are running with the ball, practise using your stick and body movements to wrong-foot your opponents.

◁ Beating an opponent when you have possession, not only requires good control, but the ability to create space. Practise looking around the field while you are dribbling. You should check the positions and movements of your team-mates and opponents before you take a pass.

The one-two pass is one of the simplest techniques for getting past an opponent. Make a short pass to a team-mate, run on past your opponent and receive a return pass. It is sometimes called the wall pass, because it is like bouncing the ball off a wall.

All players enjoy shooting goals, but it is a skill that needs to be practised. Good strikers have not only learned how to score, but also where and when to find the best opportunities. Defenders rarely leave you much time to shoot goals, so as soon as the ball is in the shooting circle, don't waste time, shoot!

▷ Many goals are scored from saves or rebounds from the goalkeeper, so always follow up a shot by coming in and looking for these further opportunities.

Game skills in defence

The aims of tackling are to break up play and to win possession of the ball. Every player must know how to tackle in order to put the opposition under pressure. Sometimes it may not be possible to win control of the ball, but at least you can try to put the ball out of play and give your team time to reorganize.

There are some general rules for good tackling. The first is to watch the ball, not your opponent's stick or body. Reducing the space available to opponents puts them under pressure. If you can, make them go past on your right or open side by leaving more space there, a technique known as channelling. Timing is important, too. Don't rush in to tackle until your opponent's stick moves away from the ball. Keep your stick on the ground.

◁ Because body and stick contact is not allowed, you must position yourself and time your tackle carefully. Here you see a reverse-stick tackle.

▷ Tackling in front of the body: the tackle should be a sudden but accurate jab, timed just as your opponent takes his or her stick away from the ball. Regain your balance and, if you have used one hand, get your right hand back on the stick as soon as you have the ball. The player on the right has successfully completed a tackle.

Open-sided tackle

You need to be well-balanced, holding the stick in your left hand. Lead with your left shoulder and foot. Go in low, eyes on the ball, knees bent, stick close to the ground. The tackler shown here on the left must take care not to hit the opponent's stick.

The reverse-side tackle

Be level or just ahead of your opponent when you tackle, holding the stick in your left hand with the toe pointing to the ground. The further away you are, the flatter the stick will be. Hook the ball away with the toe of the stick. The tackler is shown here on the right.

Goalkeeping

Quick reactions, concentration, agility, good positioning and bravery are qualities needed for the specialist job of goalkeeper. Dramatic saves keep your team in the game, but no matter how keen you are, never attempt the job without proper protection.

Low shots can be saved by bringing the pads together, with knees forward to ensure that the ball drops in front of the feet, ready to clear it. Once the ball has been controlled, it can be kicked with the instep towards the sidelines.

◁ Goalkeepers need to be well-balanced as they see the ball approaching the circle. Weight should be forward, on the balls of the feet, knees bent and feet shoulder-distance apart. The stick should be held halfway down in the right hand. The left hand stays free, ready to save any high shots.

Sometimes it is necessary to save and clear in one movement, using a combination of body motion and the rebound qualities of the pads and kickers. For wide saves, stick and hands need to be used. The goalkeeper is the only player allowed to use the stick above shoulder height to stop the ball - unless it endangers another player. Goalkeepers can make the job of shooting for goal harder by being aware of the angles available, so moving into positions that will narrow or reduce the target zone.

Right-hand saves

When saving on the right-hand side, the right hand remains on the stick, the left hand coming across, to make a wider barrier.

Left-hand saves

The left hand can be used to save shots wide to the goalkeeper's left-hand side or high. However, the goalkeeper must be sure to present a flat hand to the ball, so that it drops down and is not bounced back to the attackers.

Restarts and set plays

Every game of hockey contains a large number of stoppages and re-starts, from which the team in possession will be trying to ensure that an attack can be maintained. The defenders will be working hard to deny them such opportunities. A common feature of all set pieces is the importance of those players who are waiting for the ball. They can create space on the field, into which passes can be made.

▽ Penalty corners are awarded against defenders for deliberate offences within the 25-yard area or for accidental fouls within the shooting circle. The attackers must stand outside the circle. No more than five defenders may stand behind their goal-line.

There are a number of different re-starts, according to where and how the ball went out of play. A sideline ball is taken when a team passes the ball over a sideline. When the ball goes out of play over the goal-line from the stick of an attacker (for example, through a mis-hit at goal), a defender restarts the game from anywhere along a line from where the ball went out of play, up to the 16-yard line. Corners are awarded if a defender hits the ball over the goal-line unintentionally.

A free hit is the penalty for an offence such as rough or dangerous play, or a foul tackle. The bully re-starts play if both sides commit offences at the same time or if play has been stopped for an injury.

△ A penalty stroke is a contest between an attacker, shooting from the penalty spot, and the goalkeeper. It is awarded for a deliberate foul within the shooting circle or for an accidental offence that prevents a certain goal being scored.

Young players' hockey

Mini-hockey and colts hockey are highly competitive games that have been developed with young children in mind, to give them the excitement and action of hockey, but with fewer rules to worry about. These games are played on a smaller pitch, usually measured across the width of a full-sized playing area, by teams of not more than seven players. Mini-hockey matches consist of two halves of ten minutes each way. Colts hockey lasts longer, each half being 15 minutes long. In both games, the small pitch ensures that everyone is closely involved in the action.

△ Mini-hockey, shown here, is played with a lighter ball. There are no shooting circles - goals can be scored from anywhere in the attacking half of the pitch. Colts hockey introduces the shooting circle, the penalty corner and offside rules.

Indoor hockey is a fast and exciting version of hockey that is growing rapidly in popularity. The game is based on pushing, not hitting, the ball. A lightweight hockey stick is used. There are generally six players per side on the pitch at a time, though teams may substitute players. The game offers an excellent opportunity for young players to learn the sport.

△ For indoor hockey, the ball is the same size as for field hockey, but seamless, which allows it to move smoothly over the wooden floor.

Glossary

Back-stick
The rounded side of a hockey stick, opposite to the flat, hitting face.

Bully
A way of re-starting play after both sides in a game have committed a simultaneous offence. In a bully, two opposing players must tap their sticks on the ground, just behind the ball then against each other twice, before competing to hit the ball.

Dribble
Moving with the ball, keeping it in close contact with the stick.

Flick
A shot that is made when a ball is pushed and raised off the ground.

Free hit
After a rule infringement, play is re-started by a free hit. It is awarded to the non-offending side.

Goal-line
The part of the back line that is between the goalposts.

Halfway line
The centre-line on the pitch which is 50 yards (45 m) from each of the back lines.

Hit
A stroke made with a swinging movement of the stick in order to increase the ball's speed.

Marking
Keeping close to an opposing player to make it difficult for him or her to obtain possession of the ball.

Offside
Rule infringement. Made when a player in the opposition's 25-yard (22.9m) area receives the ball from a pass made with fewer than two members of the other side between him or her and the goal-line.

Open-side
When the stick is used on the right of your body, it is known as hitting on the open side. On the left, it is referred to as hitting on the reverse.

Pass-back
The means of starting a game or re-starting it at half-time or after a goal has been scored. The pass-back is played from the centre line.

Penalty corner
Used to be called a short corner, it is awarded against defenders for a deliberate offence within the 25-yard (22.9m) area, and accidental fouls in the shooting circle. Also if a defender plays the ball over the defence goal-line to stop an attack.

Penalty stroke
A free push or flick at goal from the penalty spot, 7 yards (6.5m) in front of the goal. Awarded for infringements in the shooting circle.

Playing distance
The distance - normally 5 yards (4.55m) - which opponents need to be from a free hit when it is taken.

Push
Moving the ball along the ground by a pushing movement, with both the ball and the head of the stick in contact with the ground.

Reverse stick
The use of the flat side of the stick, turned to face to the right.

Scoop
The name for a shovel-like shot, made to raise the ball off the ground.

Shooting circle
The semi-circle marked out on the hockey pitch, in front of each goal. In order for a goal to be scored, the ball must be inside the shooting circle 'D' when the shot is struck by a player.

Sideline ball
Means of re-starting play after the ball has been hit across a sideline.

Tackle
The act of trying to get the ball from an opponent.

Hockey Organizations

All England Women's Hockey Association
51 High Street
Shrewsbury
SY1 1ST

The Hockey Association
The Norfolk House
102 Saxon Gate West
Milton Keynes
MK9 2EP

Australian Hockey Association
Level 9
Faulkner Centre
499 St Kilda Road
Melbourne
Victoria 3004

Field Hockey Canada
802-1600 Pnom
James Naismith Drive
Gloucester
Ontario K1B SN4

New Zealand Hockey Federation
PO Box 24-024
Royal Oak
Auckland 3

Books to read

Take Up Hockey, Norman Hughes (Springfield Books Limited, 1990)
Play the Game: Hockey, Carl Ward (Ward Lock Limited, 1989)
Hockey: the Skills of the Game, John Cadman (The Crowood Press Limited, 1987)
For teachers and coaches:
Coaching Hockey, David Whitaker (The Crowood Press Limited, 1990)

Index